FACEBOOK GROUP MARKETING

For

REAL ESTATE AGENTS
and
LOAN ORIGINATORS

BY

MARTY HUMAN

AKA

MARTY BAHAMA

FACEBOOK GROUP MARKETING FOR REAL ESTATE AGENTS AND LOAN ORIGINATORS

DISCLAIMER: The content of this book is subject to change. The Publisher and the Author make no representations or warranties with respect to the accuracy or completeness of the work. This book is not intended to provide legal or financial advice. The laws and regulations for loan originators and real estate agents vary from state to state. Various policies and rules to be followed differ from company to company. The advice we provide is meant to be used with good judgement and common sense, and without express guarantees. Individual results will vary based on personal motivation, effort and skills.

FACEBOOK GROUP MARKETING FOR REAL ESTATE AGENTS
AND LOAN ORIGINATORS

As my family and friends will tell you, I have always had a desire to help people do better, especially when it comes to Real Estate. Meeting Kamikaze Kristi has enabled me to help more people than I ever imagined. We are going to teach you how to use the Facebook Groups so well that you will need to find a "Kristi" to help. (Nope, you can't have mine, LOL!)

Marty Human

Table of Contents

LUCKY DISCOVERY & NO MORE BUYING LEADS

I stumbled across the "Groups" on Facebook in 2014, thanks to my friend Wayne Palmer. He jokingly said, "Before you know it, you will be using Facebook for advertising." We had been long-time poker buddies, and he knew I had that hustler mentality.

Later that night as I was scrolling through Facebook, I found a local buy/sell/trade group with about 2,000 members. There were all sorts of posts with household items for sale, lawn care services available, and even recommendations for the best restaurants in town. As I started searching further, I came across multiple other types of groups too.

It seemed obvious to me that some of these people might need a home loan, or at least maybe at some point down the road. I created my first post that night, and I kept it simple. And guess what? It worked BETTER than I could have imagined! People were interested! They all wanted to know how I could help them get a home loan! I was getting connected with a bunch of people who actually WANTED MY HELP, and of course I helped! I already had an online application link, so it was simple to message people and let them fill it out at their own pace.

The applications began flowing in and it felt great to have so many people interested in getting a loan. I kept this amazing application-getting tool to myself at first, but the applications were practically falling from the sky! At that point, in my mind, it was all a numbers game. The more people that I connected with, the more that would apply. Then, I could just follow-up from there.

David DeWitt and I had been working together with a few loan originators in our Knoxville branch for about six months, and up until this point spending about $3k per month for leads. We had tried advertising on the radio, yard signs, print ads, etc., but none of it came close to what the Facebook Groups began doing for us! I would look at the board and count 30 loans working, and 20 of them were related to the Facebook Groups! We were able to stop buying leads, period.

After teaching our loan originators how to utilize the Facebook Groups, it didn't take long for them to start putting up serious numbers too. Most of them went from an average of 15 to 30 applications to OVER 150 applications per month! Imagine being able to close more loans than ever before, WITHOUT HAVING TO SPEND A PENNY FOR ADVERTISING OR LEADS. You simply get on Facebook, have a few conversations in Facebook Messenger, and then BOOM—you have an application in your email from a REAL PERSON WHO WANTS AND NEEDS YOUR HELP!

I feel extremely fortunate in figuring out how to utilize the Facebook Groups, and to have it actually result in an endless supply of people who want to do business. It has been such a life-changing tool! Facebook Groups are so powerful, I truly believe that if you can't make it in the business using them, then you must be lacking DRIVE. No need to sugar coat it; it's not a tough life, but you need motivation and drive with a willingness to do what it takes.

Real estate agents and loan originators take a huge step by committing to a commission-only job. To do this, you have to be your own boss, manage your own time, and know that if you do not write a contract or get that loan closed, you will not be getting a paycheck. Using Facebook, I can choose when to work and I can make as much money as I want. There is no ceiling. I can do something I love and never have to clock in, and you can too, especially now with the use of the Facebook Groups.

"Our loan originators went from an average of 15-30 applications to reeling in over 150 applications per month!"

Marty Human

IN THE BIZ

I've spent most of my life working in commission-only jobs and sales positions. I bought and sold on eBay. I did office equipment sales for a little while. I tried working as a real estate agent when I was younger—first selling golf course property, then listing and showing houses. It didn't take long for me to realize that being a real estate agent wasn't what I wanted to do! I liked having my weekends to spend more time with the family.

Joe Delbridge, a long-time friend, introduced me to the mortgage business in 2004. I immediately took to the challenge of a new career and quickly became a top producer. I was then promoted to branch manager and transferred locations several times to help grow the volume of other branches, which I always accomplished in the first few months.

The sub-prime lender I worked for shut down in 2006. I quickly bounced over to another sub-prime lender as a branch manager. I took that branch from the bottom to the top after just a couple of months. We remained on top until I was offered a branch manager position in Louisville. It was there that I had the privilege to work with Jay Smith, one of the best loan originators I know, not to mention a great friend for life.

When the market crashed in 2008, I decided to move back to Knoxville and leave the mortgage business. I got back into buying and selling, as well as playing a lot of poker! I spent a big part of my life playing poker and shooting pool. But then in 2012 the sheriff's department decided to arrest me for running a few poker games. It was at that point I decided to leave the poker world and return to mortgages!

David and I started out with a low-key office and just a couple of loan originators. We were able to move to a better location in a nicer office building, and now we have two other branches, one in Nashville and one in Greenville, SC.

We went from strictly teaching our branch how to post in groups, to now teaching real estate agents and loan originators all over the world how to use the Buzz Formula. We keep moving forward and growing very quickly, thanks to a lot of hard work and dedication from everyone!

PINEAPPLE & FAMILY

Eryka Lynn Human, aka Pineapple, was born May 28th,1999. She is my baby. I would work twelve-hour days, six days a week, just to make sure I could spoil her. Then I would stay up all night playing poker with my buddies. They would always ask me, "How can you have so much drive?" The answer was easy: "ERYKA". I want to make sure she has everything she needs to be safe and enjoy her life.

Before morphing into a Human, my last name was "King" and it influenced the crown that is now our Human Energy Buzz logo. I was adopted at a very young age after my real mother, (Shirley Jean King), was shot to death.

My Mom and Dad, also known as Sonny and Velma Human, have been a huge part of my sense of drive. I grew up with awesome older brothers and sisters (Wayne, Sandy, Tony, Eugene, and Monica). They all had an impact on the person I became. Dad always reminds me of Andy Griffith, teaching valuable life lessons and being great at everything he does.

But when I was 40, I received a strange phone call, by someone claiming to be my sister-in-law. It turned out to be true, and thanks to the dedication of Alicia Doss, I was able to meet my little brother David Doss. I say little brother only because I'm a year older. He got the height and dark skin. I clearly stole the handsome!

Now I am truly the lucky one on this planet because I have a wonderful white family and I have a wonderful black family (David's super sweet mother Mary, Dorie, Desiree, Gemari, and little David and the rest of our awesome Texas family). Neither David or I knew our real fathers, but we know Shirley was our real mother.

I'm very lucky to have such great friends and family, but I really hit the lottery when I met Kamikaze Kristi. Everything started falling into place, it truly was meant to be.

"Using the Buzz Formula combined with the Buzz Loop inside of the Facebook Groups, I can choose when to work and I can make as much money as I want, there is no ceiling."

Marty Human

KAMIKAZE KRISTI & OUR FACEBOOK GROUP EMPIRE

I got very lucky finding the Facebook Groups, but as I mentioned, I got even luckier meeting Kamikaze Kristi. I put on the best sales pitch ever to convince her to marry me! Anytime a 7 can convince a 12 to marry him, he better jump on it before she changes her mind! Honestly, I am the one that has the mouth and ambition to put wheels in motion, but Kristi is definitely smart, in addition to being very DRIVEN.

Kristi spent countless hours putting my name out there for everyone to see, and because of those connections there are now so many people living in their own home instead of renting. Not only has she changed lives in that direction, but she also taught me about text replacement! It is a game changer, because it makes messaging so much quicker and easier, especially when posting or responding on Facebook.

Kristi had been going to school to get a degree in Healthcare IT when we first met. Shortly after that, she was laid off from the doctor's office where she spent the past seven years managing their medical transcription and billing. Most of the time when people are suddenly laid off they will get upset or feel lost on how to handle the change, but not Kristi! From the beginning, she said they did her a favor. Life is definitely about timing!

Now she had some free time in her schedule to focus on school and finish her degree. It was a major accomplishment, and something she had spent several years working towards while working more than full-time and raising her son. She had the desire to be more financially stable, and with her degree and experience she could have easily moved into another medical office position and earn a comfortable salary.

But I'm a "sales guy," and thankfully one result of Kristi's layoff was us now having all this time together. She quickly saw how easy it was for me to contact people using Facebook Groups, and the ability to reel in a ton of applications. She knew we could have a comfortable income if I consistently closed loans, so she decided to "help me" with my loan originating.

Before I knew it, she was on my Facebook account as much as I was! She became completely involved in helping me generate applications. Kristi started rolling in 8 to 10 applications per day like clockwork. I actually had to ask her to slow down! The hardest part for us was simply trying to keep up with all the people applying, which was a great problem to have even if it was a bit challenging.

Imagine the snowball effect created with follow-up after having 200 people fill out an online application. Inevitably, some give an incorrect phone number, don't answer the phone, or even respond to emails. But we just kept saying, "How can we complain about too much business?"

We are one of the top-performing mortgage branches. Loan originators, real estate agents, and other self-employed folks reach out to me daily to get advice on how to improve their business by using Facebook Groups. It's crazy to think how fast this has escalated, when at one time I thought it was crazy that Kristi still kept joining group after group.

Now we have groups, mostly in the five different states our branches cover, that we have exclusive admin rights in with over two million members. We have been training loan originators and real estate agents how to generate business on Facebook by using the groups for leverage, all while creating Facebook Messenger Groups for easy communication and follow-up.

If not for the amazing Kamikaze Kristi, we wouldn't be where we are today. She spent time surfing through the groups and reading different group rules to make sure we weren't doing something that would get us kicked out or blocked. And then she spent many more hours researching on Google to get extra tips and learn the ins and outs of Facebook and the Groups.

"Since I began using the Facebook Groups, I have not had the pressure of wondering where I am going to find my next client, and it is such an amazing feeling."

Marty Human

BUSINESS PAGES vs GROUPS & LEAD GEN

As a loan originator, there have always been three distinct ways to make money in the mortgage business. The way that used to work best for me was to CALL LEADS. We would buy leads from various big companies (as would other lenders), and we usually paid a set amount per lead.

A LEAD was really just the name and phone number of a person who had expressed interest in obtaining a home loan. That's it... Not much more information to go on, so it took some definite sales skills when calling LEADS. It was a tough task of convincing them you were a professional, why you were calling, and then getting that application! I would make 100 calls a day and turn on all the sales charm and persuasion I could dig out. I would end up with about three to four applications. Out of these, I could usually figure one good deal.

The second way to find business was to go out and buy dozens of donuts and hit the streets, driving to different realty offices and hoping you could find a real estate agent that you could convince to send you business. There are many obvious issues with this approach in my opinion, and the biggest one is that many loan originators are not confident enough to be able to walk in and win referrals from people who are already sending all their business to SOMEONE ELSE.

If you are lucky enough to find a real estate agent who isn't sending their business to a particular lender, and they agree to send you referrals, you now have another challenge of keeping this agent happy. It's not easy when borrowers have financial complications that appear during the course of underwriting. If the approval for the loan becomes uncertain the loan originator is suddenly under pressure to explain why, or "fix it". If there are repeated problems, then you begin worrying that they might start sending the borrowers to another lender. Agents similar concerns. The last thing anyone wants is for their client to be redirected to someone else.

The third way to get applications was just "normal" word of mouth—friends, family, etc. I did a few loans each year as a result of referrals from people I knew, but not enough to want to let that be the way I made a living. Honestly, I have always felt like friends and family were the hardest loans to get done. Some people do all their business this way, but I usually felt like they were a lot more pressure. Everyone has a story to tell about their personal mortgage experience, and usually it has made them a sort of expert on the topic of mortgages, at least in their own mind and it becomes an extra hurdle for the loan originator to manage.

In order to generate leads and more business, both big and small companies are using the typical Facebook Business Page with paid advertisements to drive traffic. For a business to show up in the news feed for any Facebook user, there is a complex process of creating and running advertisements, which are then shown based on Facebook's secret algorithms.

A Facebook Group is quite different because of the personal connections with all the new people constantly requesting to become members. A Facebook Group gives you greater ability to interact with current and future clients, in part because it is so simple to get started and continue using. It does a lot of the advertising because of the ways that Facebook highlights common connections.

When we began creating Personal Branding Groups (PBG) we discovered another way to increase business, faster and easier than we could have imagined possible. We have figured out how to show up in the feeds of more potential clients, and how to advertise without advertising, by using the Facebook Groups for personal branding.

"Whether you are a real estate agent or loan originator, with the use of the Facebook Groups you will get your name out there better than ever."

Marty Human

FACEBOOK JAIL & FACEBOOK MESSENGER TIMEOUT

Years ago, when the Facebook Groups were smaller, it seemed like they were more micromanaged by Facebook. But as time has gone on, most of the control of what happens in the groups has been left up to the admins and moderators. This is important, because as you can imagine Facebook does not like to let people advertise for free.

In fact, Facebook is quick to provide consequences if they think you are being abusive or doing something that violates their terms. I'm not sure how I even managed to keep pushing after the first time in "Facebook Jail." Keep in mind, this is just the terminology we commonly use, but it means being blocked from joining, posting, or commenting in the groups. Everything else about your Facebook account, outside of the groups, is completely normal.

In the beginning, when we were blocked from the groups Facebook did not inform us how long the ban would last. I remember when we first got blocked, it felt like an eternity because they wouldn't give us a notice of how long our "sentence" would be. There were even a couple of loan originator trainees who quit because they had been put in Facebook Jail and they just didn't have what it took to call leads.

Thankfully, Facebook is now better about letting us know how long we will be blocked. In the Help Center section is the Support Inbox, which is where they will send a message that gives a time and date of when your ban will be over. We've found that Facebook Jail will usually last anywhere from twenty-four hours to fourteen days. There is also what we term "Facebook Probation" which (to us) means you are blocked from posting in any of the groups, unless you are an admin of the group.

We consider "Facebook Purgatory" when Facebook deactivates your account. Even if someone on Facebook searches for you, they won't be able to see that you were ever on there, and they can't message you. When you make your living by messaging people on Facebook, you can imagine the state of anxiety this could cause!

Facebook "Messenger Timeout" typically involves either messaging too many people or messaging them too fast. This normally lasts anywhere from four to twenty-four hours. Many people who are new to using the Facebook Groups will be a little too eager and end up in Facebook Timeout, so they find it helpful to use our Buzz Team group for answers and feedback. Usually we can say, "Oh, yes, that's no big deal. You were probably doing something that caused a red flag."

And, of course, the answer is always along the lines of, "Yes, I posted in a ton of groups today." Or, they will admit to posting in a bunch of groups very quickly. Facebook doesn't mind if you start discussions and interact in a group, but when you're posting fast in too many groups, or doing something out of character, they will stop you for a moment to make sure you aren't spamming or possibly a fake account.

Some people take right to this system. Previously, they never would have taken the risk of posting in Facebook Groups, because they felt like they were intruding. But, we have already learned what to do and what not to do with the groups, and we have a pretty good idea of how to avoid getting in trouble. Admins of groups will usually limit the number of promotional posts, such as stock photos and pictures of fancy homes. They normally don't have an issue with discussions, especially in larger groups.

After all these years of posting and building, we have been hit with all kinds of obstacles to overcome! When we first went through Facebook Jail and Facebook Messenger Timeout, it would have been helpful to know that this was normal and what to expect. If only we knew what to avoid doing, we wouldn't repeat it!

I would consider some of the more valuable information I have about Facebook Groups to be our experiences concerning what you can do and what you cannot do when posting. We know it is possible to get blocked for any number of offenses, such as adding too many members to groups in a short period of time. We know there are limits to how many times per day you should post, how many groups you should post in, how many messages you can send, how many people you can tag in your posts, and how many times you can share posts.

Now that we have a better understanding of the dos and don'ts, everyone is posting in Facebook Groups and messaging future clients at all hours of the day and night, growing their business. Between creating a PBG, and being a member in other groups, along with the help of Facebook Messenger and the Buzz Loop, we no longer need to spend every minute talking on the phone and we definitely don't need to buy leads!

"After spending years of working in the Facebook Groups, we have a few tips and tricks to avoid Facebook Jail and Facebook Messenger Timeout."

Marty Human

GAME CHANGERS & TEXT REPLACEMENT

Kristi and I have only been together for a few years, but in that time we have had what we call game changing moments. May of 2015 was a game changer because we got married, and at the same time Kristi finished her degree. This gave her a lot of freedom and time to focus on our new life together and make sure our kids were both happy with their new living situation!

When Kristi first started paying attention to what I was doing on Facebook, the first thing she said was, "Quit re-typing all of your posts over and over." She had been using TEXT REPLACEMENT for years in her job as a medical transcriptionist, and she knew the value of being able to type quickly!

One very important step is learning how to set up and use text replacement on your phone. The iPhone has a built-in feature in the settings section. Some Android phones have a similar setting, but there is an app called "Texpand" in the Google Play Store which is much easier to use for creating shortcuts. https://play.google.com/store/apps/details?id=com.isaiasmatewos.texpandpro

TEXT REPLACEMENT allows you to pre-program a phrase to any abbreviation you prefer. It is recommended that you start your abbreviations with "zz." For example, I have a shortcut for my application website so that when I type "zzapp," followed by a space, my phone will automatically put www.southwestfunding.com/mhuman/apply-now/. This saves me from having to type the actual website address.

The potential to save time is enormous! All the repetitive and difficult-to-type phrases can be abbreviated to whatever shortcut is easiest to remember, and then you don't have to worry about typos and grammar checks. Just make sure it is right the first time, and it will be right every time!

Having these shortcuts on my phone has changed everything. Planning what to say in advance was definitely a game changer! I was spending a lot of time re-typing posts, repeatedly typing in the same answers to different people, and using a ton of copy/paste. With text replacement I can just remember a shortcut for my "standard response" and type that abbreviation instead.

I don't have to try to think about exactly how to phrase my answers when I am busy multitasking, and I don't have to worry about appearing careless. Plenty of times when messaging my phone "auto-corrected" the wrong way and I didn't realize it until after the send button was pushed! This tool has been a GAME CHANGER for everyone we have taught it to!

Even better was reducing the number of difficult phone calls that would wear on my nerves—calls where the person had a bad connection, or their accent made them difficult to understand. Most of these issues were eliminated simply by using Facebook Messenger for communicating. This helped keep me organized and on track with my clients about the items they needed in order to complete the loan process.

"Text Replacement has been a GAME CHANGER for everyone and goes together like peanut butter and jelly with the Facebook Groups."

Marty Human

MAKING THE PROCESS EASY

Facebook gave most of the group control to the Admins, and many of the groups have grown tremendously. I have noticed that membership gains are like a snowball effect and Facebook Groups that had 15K members five years ago have close to 60K members now. The bigger they get, the faster they grow!

My groups with 10K members normally gain around 20 to 40 new members each day, and my groups with 60K members usually gain around 100 members per day. The more they grow, the better the opportunity for us to create leverage and generate more business.

Kristi was all about creating a standard process from the very beginning. She kept reminding me that we should pay attention to the ways we could simplify or eliminate the more time-consuming and difficult tasks. She has a very different brain. I tell her this all the time! In figuring out how to streamline what I was doing, we were able to show struggling loan originators what they needed in order to be consistently producing.

We use Google Sheets to keep track of the Facebook Groups we have joined and the ones we Admin. I recommend keeping track of your favorite groups, and any groups you create, at a minimum. Once we have loaded the client names into the Google Sheets, we start color coordinating each line depending on the status of the buying process. This helps us stay on top of the next step. At the end of each month we wind up with a sheet full of all these different colors, and it makes it so much easier to identify where each client stands with just a glance.

Together, Kristi and I went from being in 150 groups, to over 7,000. Facebook Groups are more powerful than ever because of the tools available for group admins, and I can see how they keep making changes and continue to get better with each app update. They are constantly adjusting the layout and function of different aspects within the groups, and we are always thinking about new ways we can utilize the tools available. Zuckerberg even announced during a worldwide conference, that they have switched their direction from connecting friends and family to focusing on bringing communities and people together using the Facebook Groups.

"You gain LEVERAGE by being in control of Facebook Groups, and they continue to grow."

Marty Human

VALUE & ALGORITHMS

I realized the Facebook Groups had gained an incredible amount of value when Facebook started allowing us to ask potential new members three "screening" questions before we let them in the group. This was HUGE!

Imagine having a group with 10K or 20K members, and every day an average of 30 to 50 people asking to join. This means that every day people see your three questions. This tool is intended to help Admins in quickly screening new members and see who they want to allow into the group. When you really think about it, the value here is truly enormous! And this is just a starting point of how to utilize Facebook Groups.

There are many different ways to use the groups to find clients. One common question I get is, "Will we oversaturate these groups?" There is no shot of this happening in my opinion. Groups are growing at crazy speeds, and no matter where you are, there are literally hundreds of thousands of groups around for people to join and participate in. Plus, the Facebook algorithms and features keep changing and improving, ultimately affecting everyone.

I found it hard to believe when I heard loan originators complain about a lack of applications, and then blame it on too many other loan originators posting! I reminded them that Kristi is in thousands of groups, and not once did she have trouble getting applications. There were instances where it looked like loan originators were posting on top of one another, and a few of them got bent out of shape, until they paid closer attention and realized they were not posted close to the same time at all! It only appeared that way in their own notifications.

The posts work on algorithms which, simply stated, means that just because you post in a group with 25K members it doesn't mean that all the members will immediately see that post. If you are Facebook friends with some other people who are using the groups for business the same way, then you will likely see a lot of similar posts more often. That is simply because of your common connections, but it doesn't mean that the posts repeatedly show up that way for anyone else who happens to be looking at Facebook.

Facebook's algorithm determines which posts will show in the personal feed for each individual also based on their profile settings and search history. For example, if your post contains the word "house", AND if a member in that group has searched for or clicked on anything to do with a house, then there is a chance that person will see your post!

"One of the biggest keys to my success as a loan originator has always been my DRIVE. If you want to make six figures, all it takes is the Buzz Formula combined with DRIVE."

Marty Human

THE BUZZ FORMULA & IMMEDIATE RESULTS

Every day the momentum grows. The ways we have embraced social media technology and communication put us at the front of the curve. We have a prime opportunity to enjoy huge growth and rewards, because we are ahead of the game. We already have loan originators and real estate agents getting great results and closing plenty of loans as a result of using the Buzz Formula on Facebook.

We have been working out a process to make it easy for anyone to follow because it produces IMMEDIATE RESULTS. We wanted it to be rewarding for people to follow the BUZZ FORMULA! In fact, it even becomes a little bit addicting for most people to see how many responses and applications they can generate! It doesn't take long to realize that while there is some effort and time involved, it's not hard work to do. It's easy to see the potential to have a very good income, more than enough to support a family.

Another lesson Kristi taught me was the importance of paying attention and working smarter. She noticed that while we were supposedly in a seller's market, the contract amounts coming in were even lower than the median home prices. She said, "You know, I don't like the fact that we are averaging such small loan amounts." I said, "Well, heck, neither do I! It's simple math to me. If I do a $200K loan, it's like doing two loans in one!"

Then she said, "Well, I'm going to increase our loan amounts." I'm pretty sure I spewed Coke Zero out of my mouth and said, "Good luck with that miracle, and let me know how that works out for you!"

Fast forward a couple months, and sure enough, our applications consistently were requesting larger loan amounts and we began sending pre-approvals for more than what we had been averaging. It was great to have this kind of improvement because we had been stuck in a rut of $50k to $85k loans. I looked at the posts she had been using, and nothing looked different there. So I said to her, "Ok, miracle worker. What have you done to pull this off?"

She said it was simple. Where I had focused mostly on posting basically around the area I grew up in East Tennessee, she had started expanding out further and joining groups all across the state. The branch is licensed for the entire state, and there was nothing stating I couldn't originate loans in Middle TN or West TN just as easily as I could here in East TN. She kept joining new groups in areas I never even heard of and started posting in areas that I had never worked in! But heck, we handled everything over the phone and by email anyway, and it made sense because as she joined more groups and posted in all of the different areas, she made new connections. We were now getting applications submitted by people who wanted our help from all over the state!

Typically, the mortgage business slows down a bit around the holidays, but in January 2017, while the rest of the branch complained they didn't have enough applications, I was swamped! It was definitely time to train the rest of the branch and give specific instructions on how to get applications rolling in. Some of the loan originators had been attempting to copy a bit of what we were doing, but none of them had jumped in and embraced it fully yet.

Kristi and I were still getting between 180 and 200 applications per month, and we were sure that the rest of our loan originators could replicate this. We encouraged them to tweak our scripts slightly to fit them and hoped they would follow our lead and utilize the groups. We showed them how to find groups and post in them. We taught them exactly what to say to people in Facebook Messenger, how to handle different questions, and what to expect when using Facebook Messenger to communicate.

It didn't take long for everyone to realize that we already had the ball rolling, and it was beneficial for them to follow the same path because it WORKED! We were no longer concerned with buying leads or having enough business. We were training our loan originators to make connections with people and get applications in an easier way than ever before!

Kristi came up with one great post looking for people who were living in the house they wanted to buy, and she managed to pick up a client for me within 5 minutes of posting it! We closed his loan (over $250,000!) and he came back to us a year later when he decided to move. We were able to get another loan closed for him and it was over $400,000! We went from closing $23M in volume in 2016 and increased 50% to almost $35M in volume in 2017, without buying leads!

"It becomes a little bit addicting for most people to see how many responses and applications they can generate!"

Marty Human

A COMIC BOOK & LIFE CHANGES

Kristi and I were heading to the airport on our way to Mexico for a little company-sponsored getaway for top producers, when she happened to notice a new Facebook notification and said, "This person just archived this group. I wonder if that means he doesn't want it anymore?"

The group was in Franklin County, TN. I live in Tennessee, but I had no clue at that moment exactly where this place was. But what I did know was that the group had 10K members and it would be a VERY STRONG move to be the Admin in control of such a large group!

I reached out to the guy who owned it and asked, "Would you be interested in getting rid of the Facebook Group that you just archived?"

He said, "Sure, send me a comic book, and you can have it!" It turned out that he wanted Mutants #98, which contains

Deadpool's first appearance. I got on eBay, bought it and had it shipped directly to him. On the last day we were in Mexico, he received the comic book and made me sole Admin of the group. That is when LIFE CHANGED!

Up until that point I had several smaller groups which I had grown, and the 2,500 member Knoxville Homes For Sale/Rent group, but nothing close to the 10,000 in this one. I was amazed that I could so easily have control of a group with this number of members!

The potential to generate more business was exciting and I went on a little spree acquiring more groups. In a very short period and we gained admin control of so many groups that it was hard to keep up with them. All of these groups also gave us a non-stop stream of admin tasks, such as approving members and monitoring posts.

Kristi once again came up with an amazing idea. She suggested that since I was a former real estate agent, I had a perfect opening to start partnering with agents and allow them to help me run the groups. This created a win/win situation!

"I went from having admin control of one Facebook Group with 2,500 members, to having admin control of Facebook Groups in five different states with over two million members combined."

Marty Human

OLD SCHOOL ADVERTISING & SOCIAL MEDIA

Take some advice from a former real estate agent, loan originator, branch manager, and now Facebook Group Guru, your days of paying for leads and door knocking are finished! The days of holding open houses and having no one show up are completely unnecessary. Signs in the yard, well, let's be honest, the signs may never go away! But Facebook Groups are the most powerful form of advertising I have ever seen. I have watched them grow and change so much.

By the time you set up a table at an open house and wait for possible clients to show up, you could have already reached out to hundreds of thousands of people and been carrying on many conversations at once. One thing you cannot do well in person, is carry on multiple conversations at the same time.

It is, however, not too difficult to pull that off when you are talking to people through Facebook Messenger. We are able to connect and "have conversations" with so many people at the same time! What worked 10 years ago may have been perfect then, but don't keep living in the past! There is a much easier way to do it now. We have been able to close as many deals a month as we want, because of utilizing the Facebook Groups to essentially reach an unlimited number of people. Facebook even does a lot of the hard work for us by keeping track of everything.

Life has never been so good for a real estate agent or loan originator! We can literally start a conversation with someone, then quit talking, and yet still know what's going on if we pick that conversation up again six months from now. It's especially easy when all we have to do to refresh our memory is scroll up and start reading!

We began to realize we could give people a little advice on things they could do to improve their chances when it was time for them to apply for a mortgage, and they would actually go about their lives taking our advice and come back to talk to us again when they felt ready to move forward. And guess what? Plenty of people actually do come back!

Kristi talked to thousands of people who were nowhere near being ready to buy a house. But she put in the couple of minutes it took to send them a message about the things they could do to improve their chances. This was like an investment towards future paychecks.

I have people come back to me every single day that I haven't even taken an application on yet, just because I sent them a message about some of the steps they could take to improve their situation and get a home loan in the future, and because I assured them that I would be in the business for a long time. I let them know I would be there whenever they were ready.

One key we try to remember, is that this is SOCIAL media! We are dealing with actual people, and one thing that they are looking for is a great personal reference from a legit person whom you have helped. It is a good idea to find people who can do a good job "tooting your horn," and ask them to help spread the word or occasionally be your "cheerleader" when they see your name or your posts on Facebook. People LOVE to do this, especially your past clients who are now homeowners! It doesn't take long to build up a nice stack of awesome references and proof posts.

Part of my success as a loan originator has been my confidence in talking to people. For people who don't have the "gift of gab",

Facebook Messenger is valuable because it helps them overcome any awkwardness involved in those first conversations. The level of communication is what sets apart the good and the great in terms of sales. Great communication eliminates most issues, and when we began effectively using Facebook Messenger, we gained another valuable tool.

Kristi and I spent over four years posting on Facebook to generate applications and learning about the many ways we could advertise without advertising. We were very successful, but it wasn't always rainbows and flowers! As I mentioned before, there are certain actions that will get you in trouble and even booted off Facebook and we have spent a lot of time figuring out exactly which actions cause problems.

But the truth is, that even during the times we had problems and couldn't use Facebook to "advertise," we were already in contact with so many people the occasions where we couldn't post actually gave us a needed break to get caught up!

POSITIVE REFERENCES & POSITIVE PEOPLE

I remember one of the first loans I closed from a Facebook post. The client was previously turned down by her real estate agent's usual lender. The client saw my post and said, "Hey, what the heck, I've already been turned down, so why not give it a shot?" I spoke with her on the phone for about 30 minutes, then I had her sending documents in for confirmation and gave her the pre-approval letter.

The agent called me the next day, telling me I was getting her client's hopes up, and it would be my fault when she ended up disappointed. I told her, "Look, it's simple. I can get this loan done." She said, "It's impossible. If my guy can't get it done, then it can't get done." She started laughing and hung up on me! It was to the point where the client called me, crying, and she asked me to please reassure her that I wasn't getting her hopes up for nothing! I told her not to worry, because I was going to make it happen, and that is exactly what I did.

This client ended up getting on Facebook to give me a great reference. She even mentioned in the post that she had a 580 credit score and I had completed her loan with a 4.5% rate (a true miracle). That was a solid reference and a huge factor in convincing people who weren't sure if they should trust me.

That one reference post has been responsible for many of my loans from Facebook. I have plenty of proof to show when I get the question, "Is this a scam?" There was a post from another client who said she had been turned down by five other lenders, and then WE got her loan closed! Whenever we get a great post, we take a screenshot and then share it. These screenshots really help to reassure people who don't know us.

It's all about how you turn people around and get them over to your side. I always respond with positive proof. Of course, that's not to say there isn't the occasional bit of drama that will show up on a post and try to cause problems, but Facebook has given us the option to delete offensive comments from posts and block people who are trying to create issues for others. Stay positive and just delete the negative people! That is the best way to handle negativity on your posts when it occasionally happens.

"It's all about how you turn people around and get them over to your side, and I always respond with positive proof."

Marty Human

TIMING & DIFFERENTIATION

There was an agent who reached out to me a few months after we really got going with posting in the groups who asked, "Marty, how are you advertising on Facebook?"

I told her, "Basically, I post in groups, and as people like and comment on my posts, I reach out to them and get the process started." When I was doing this, I had more business than I could handle. She was very unfamiliar with Facebook Groups, so I added her to some, taught her how to join a few, and showed her which kind to join.

She posted in some of the groups for about a week. Then I gave her a call, and said, "How did you do?" She replied, "I didn't have any luck at all. I posted every day but got zero likes and zero comments."

I responded, "Okay, I'm going to text you a post I want you to use. See how it works for you."

I already knew she didn't have any luck because I was watching some of her posts and could see the problem. She did what most real estate agents and loan originators do. They post a fancy picture of a house that very few people can afford, or they use stock photos of fancy gold keys. All of this says "I'm a real estate agent, or I'm a loan originator. Look at me."

There are real estate agents and loan originators around any corner. You must find a way to differentiate yourself from the pack. The post I sent her to use read, "Hey, everyone! I am a local real estate agent, and I finally found a lender who can go down to a 580 credit score FHA and 600 score USDA. Who is ready to get pre-approved for a home loan?"

I didn't realize it at the time but while we were talking on the phone, she used the post I sent her in a local yard sale group. All of the sudden she said, "Wow, I just got a message."

I said, "Huh?"

She replied, "Yes, I posted what you sent me just now." And that fast, she already had a message! We then sent that person an application link, he filled it out, and six weeks later we closed on a $180K loan.

I had another agent make his first post at 8 p.m., and by the next morning he had already referred over 20 clients to me! If this wasn't a game changer, I wouldn't pour my heart into it like I do. It is really exciting to find something so incredibly effective that the results are almost guaranteed! I could make plenty of money as a branch manager and just keep this information within my branches, but it is so much bigger than any of us can really imagine, and IT JUST KEEPS GROWING!

Most agents and loan originators I speak with usually do printed materials, Zillow marketing, or paid Facebook advertising. Otherwise, they rely on word of mouth. One thing these professionals have in common is a Facebook Business Page. This is where I consider myself lucky, because while everyone else was building their Facebook Pages, I was creating Facebook Groups and Personal Branding Groups (PBG).

I created a PBG called Knoxville Homes For Sale/Rent Home Buying Made Easy By Marty Human, and immediately added 100 of my friends, previous clients, and some family members. Today my group has 5K members in it and grows every day without me having to do anything to help it grow. Almost everyone that requests to join the group is in the market to either buy, sell, or rent.

"While everyone else was building their Facebook Business Pages, I was creating Facebook Personal Branding Groups."

Marty Human

POSTS WITH LIKES & COMMENTS

A group gets created and members get added to it. Then the Admin will decide who can post in the group and create rules about the types of posts that are allowed, the frequency that people can post, etc. Depending on the group type, if items are posted for sale, they will usually correspond to whatever the group name is. Typically, other members are permitted to comment on or like posts but there are some groups that have rules regarding that as well. Unless a post is deemed to specifically go against Facebook Terms and gets removed, the group Admin has the authority to allow or remove any post. They are allowed to set the rules they want, and they can allow or deny membership to anyone.

Once an item gets posted it will remain in place until another item gets posted. You usually won't see a lot of activity until you have a good number of people within the group. It just depends on the group type. As the posts start moving in the group, they trickle down and down as people post, but an amazing thing happens when someone likes or comments on a post. It boosts that particular post right back to the top!

The posts do not stay in chronological order. We have had posts pop back up that were three years old! Then, out of the blue someone saw the post, shared it, or commented, "Yes I want more information." Obviously, when this happens your post starts generating interest and advertising for you all over again. Consistently joining new groups is a great goal that we still work on! I think you should ask to join any group that pertains to your business or the areas surrounding where you live, at a minimum.

There is a lot of great advice about posts that get responses in our Buzz Team group. Sometimes we have people that feel like they aren't getting the responses they expected when they post, but usually a quick look at what they are posting will reveal the issue. It might be time to change your tactics, but the advice I give everyone is, "Don't try to reinvent the wheel!" Do what you see working. You will learn how to get plenty of likes and comments, and how to turn them into clients for life.

A wise professor once said, "To have a super successful business, you must either be first at whatever it is you are doing, or you must differentiate yourself from the competition." I think we have done just that with our approach to utilizing discussion posts in the groups about buying or selling a home.

"We have seen our POSTS popping back up three years after we initially posted them. Advertising for us for FREE."

Marty Human

PERSONAL BRANDING GROUP & THE FUTURE

Alan Thurman, one of my loan originators, asked me, "What is one thing you really regret and wish you would have done differently in your mortgage career?" Honestly, the one thing I regret not doing a good job of is keeping track of all the clients' names, numbers, and addresses that I worked with.

I was always very lazy about trying to reach out to my previous clients to ask for referrals, even though we all know those referrals are usually good as gold. If you can get them qualified, they are likely already comfortable with you and know what to expect. I intermittently had ambitions of doing a better job with keeping track, but life is busy, and it kept falling further down on my list of priorities.

The easiest way to solve this problem was sitting right in front of me the entire time. When I first created my PBG I invited some of my previous clients, friends and family to join and in the first day after I created the group, I got a referral from it! I couldn't believe it, and at the same time I was kicking myself in the rear for not making the group sooner. If I had created the group five years ago and put in every person who asked me about how to get a home loan or showed interest in my posts, I can't imagine how big it would be today! Definitely in the tens of thousands.

This has now become my personal referral center, and it helps keep my name at the top of everyone's mind when it comes time to move or refinance. There are so many different tactics to take and things to do inside the group to get these potential future clients interacting. Everyone I put in there was very receptive and happy to be involved. I began encouraging my loan originators to create their own PBGs. I explained to them that it was like taking some of the fish out of the ocean and dropping them into your personal pond.

One agent in particular that I know had been active in the groups and running a large one, and she was making six figures per year from utilizing Facebook! Imagine the opportunity to be in control of multiple groups. The potential to make a lot of money is crazy, especially when compared to door knocking or handing business cards out everywhere, hoping someone might call you one day.

There are multiple ways to "farm" groups, and even more options for admins or moderators of a group. They might not be ready to buy a home right now, but odds are that in the future they will be ready, and they will know who to go see about getting a home loan! I also began creating PBGs for everyone we were working with, so they would also benefit from having a personal pond to use for growing their business.

With the Facebook Groups and time management, it's possible to reach several thousand REAL people every day. It doesn't take long to generate a list of people who are ready to buy now and a different list of those who are working on getting ready for a future purchase. It is great to be able to wake up, post on Facebook ready to work, then have a few discussions with people that eventually result in more business. The best part about social media is that people will often share their stories and encourage others to come to us for help as well! There have been many times people came to me after working with another lender who either wasn't able to help or quoted high rates and closing costs, and they are super impressed.

Some of our strongest supporters have even been those people who were ultimately not approved for a loan, but they knew that we did everything we could to help them. They appreciated it, and let others know about the positive ways in which we work with people. The more you do, the better the testimonials you will receive. In the loan originator world, any number of seemingly small problems can become big issues. People get upset, and the reality is that mortgages, moving, and finances can all be emotional and sensitive topics for people. Sometimes there are hiccups and bumps with drama and problems to be somehow smoothed over. Communication is the key to keeping everyone at least somewhat sane!

Great communication usually eliminates most issues, or at the very least identifies them at a point in the process when they might be more easily addressed. When we began to utilize Facebook Messenger groups, we found the level of frustration and the number of telephone calls dropped because everyone was in the Buzz Loop. The Messenger groups also put people on the spot and give them a sense of urgency, because everyone can see when a message has been read and who read it. Facebook Messenger has become our best friend.

ATMOSPHERE & SUCCESS

People are posting and messaging about home buying at all hours of the day and night. I love it, because if that's as hard as we have to work to generate income, then hand me a pick, and let's start digging for gold! I tell my loan originators to enjoy life as much as they can. We are able to be mobile, and it doesn't hurt to take a few minutes here and there to jump in to work as needed. We keep working on ways to make life easier.

I tell our loan originators that they don't work FOR us, they work WITH us, and hopefully we can all work as a TEAM. One way we have helped our loan originators is by hiring great processors who are getting loans closed because we trained them on how to effectively communicate with clients through the Facebook Messenger Groups. The processor then enables the loan originator to spend more time actually originating new business!

We also taught our loan originators to quit calling leads and pounding the pavement delivering doughnut bribes. Instead, they utilize Facebook to generate more business. They have the ability to reach an unlimited number of people during the course of their day, when in the past, they were limited by the fact that they could only speak to one person at a time. Not to mention the fact that their advertising reach was much smaller and more expensive!

Now, the next step is the loan originators who admin Facebook groups teaching real estate agents how to generate new business by simply posting and starting discussions. We teach them how to ask questions and determine where in the process each new contact is, and how to provide directions from there using specific scripts. The entire process is intended to keep everyone on the same page by using the Messenger groups to make communicating easier.

The loan originators are teaching the agents to post and helping them build their PBGs, while they are sending screened applicants for us to work with. In the end, we all have the ultimate gift of increase in business. An added benefit our office has certainly noticed is the decrease in the amount of phone calls they have had to handle since everyone started using Buzz Loop Messenger groups.

I've brought in a ton of agents who have learned the Buzz Formula and I get contacted every day by others who have heard about it and want to learn more. We recently developed a system called Buzz Formula Nation, which is where we have multiple Buzz Team Members posting for each other and working the comments in tandem. Typically in the mortgage business the November-January time of year is a bit slower, but we are so busy and have so many people who want our help that we could work 24/7 and never get done! Everyone posts in the groups and then send me screenshots of the posts with multiple comments and likes. One agent's very first post got 700 comments and over 100 likes, as well as shares by several people.

One of the hardest things for us was trying to figure out who had applied and keeping track of which applications we could expect from the Facebook group comments. Even though we had the applications coming straight to our emails, we became so busy that we needed a system for organizing them. It would also add to the confusion when people would say they were going to fill out an application, but sometimes not follow through. The great part about using Facebook is that we still have the Messenger connection, so we can re-contact people who were interested.

"Our processors are able to carry on so many more conversations, without making phone calls, thanks to Facebook Messenger Groups."

Marty Human

TIME TO HIRE & TRAIN FOR GREAT RESULTS

We are still in the early stages of realizing the benefits of the Facebook Groups. It wasn't that long ago that Facebook redirected their focus to the groups, and the word is getting out. They make changes every day with new features and options to use. The improvements have created more opportunities to connect than we have ever seen before! I have had so many people tell me they love the amazing communication we have created with Facebook Messenger and it's the reason why they choose to work with us. It's definitely valuable, because I remember being a real estate agent back in the day and how much I hated not being kept in the loop!

I hired a few people to help us with all the applications we had coming in. We kept stressing the importance of maintaining a database, because the connections we gain from the groups are an investment in future business. One way we attempt to keep up is by using Google Sheets, which I feel is much easier to use than Microsoft Excel.

I even held training sessions for the agents in my Buzz Team group who wanted to learn what we were doing, some of whom drove five hours to my office. Then, Kristi convinced me to try Google Hangouts. Now I do most training through ZOOM and within the Buzz Team Group, where I go LIVE normally five days a week at 10pm eastern. We keep evolving!

I have talked to many real estate agents who have a Facebook Group with five or ten thousand members, but they don't have a clue how to utilize it. They could be getting more listings, more loan applications, or whatever other aspect of their business that needs a boost. One of the simplest ways is to simply treat your group as a blog.

As an agent or a loan originator, a PBG can be used to start simple conversations every day. There are also other ways to take advantage, for example, changing the three questions asked to new members who request to join. Or, use the group by posting all of your listings and any new, hot houses that hit the market. If you aren't interested in using the group as a blog, you can still use it as a holding pond for all the people you talk to out there, especially the ones that "aren't ready yet."

You can also create polls to spark discussions and find people who didn't realize how you can help them. It is smart to add

FACEBOOK GROUP MARKETING FOR REAL ESTATE AGENTS
AND LOAN ORIGINATORS

coworkers to your group and let them share their listings. But remember, this is your group! As the Admin, you can control what's posted by setting up the group so that you have to approve every member post in the group. That way, you can decide what stays and what goes.

The Facebook Groups have admin tools and group insights to help track statistics. As an admin, you can look at any member and track their Facebook participation level. If you are the boss tracking your team's performance, you will definitely want to become familiar with group insights. When one of my loan originators says he/she is having issues getting applications, we can take a look at the group insights and then usually we can say, "Well, here is the obvious problem."

One of the bigger groups I admin is in Nashville, Tennessee. It has around 59K members, up very quickly from the 36K it had when I initially took it over. These are members that might get to see my name, telephone number, and anything else I want them to see. Approximately 70 new people each day for the rest of your life will see my info. It's almost like being at a full-time home show without spending all day sitting at one. These shows may have 25K people roll through, but that doesn't mean they will all stop to talk or see the information.

Think about the last time you held or went to an open house for a listing, and the time this involved. Now, instead of physically holding open houses, you can create events within groups including a description about a specific property.

Or, imagine your group having 50K members, and creating an event such as a "First-Time Home Buying" class. Treat this group like a daily blog, and it could generate enough interest to create the event again every month! I have had some people get their personal group built up to over 1,000 members in the first weekend. Some people who use our posting system haven't started a PBG yet because the posting works so well that branding doesn't seem like a priority. We just happen to be on a mission to help everyone around us make a ton of money! Now I need some more help, but as I always say, "it's a marathon, not a sprint!"

"Now, instead of door knocking, going to trade shows, or wasting hours at open houses, it's easy to quickly generate far more business from the comfort of your own home."

Marty Human

THE BUZZ LOOP & LESS STRESS

I have been preaching for the last few years that Facebook Messenger is the most powerful tool we can use for communication. It is literally life changing! We can introduce everyone involved and communicate between the loan originators, agents, clients, processors, etc., coordinating so that everyone stays on the same page.

Facebook Messenger has allowed us to contact people and have further conversations about the home buying and loan pre-approval process because it provides a direct link to that person forever! Then, once a client is pre-qualified, we add our processors to the conversation so they can introduce themselves and assist with the entire approval process and obtain the items needed.

This is valuable because there is a direct line of communication for everyone to access in order to ask questions and receive updates. Lack of communication will never be a problem again. It creates a sense of urgency but is less stressful because it updates when each person has read a message. Most of the time, people respond more quickly than if the exchange were to happen by email or phone, and it also helps keep the message clear. Now we can be proactive by directing contacts on Facebook to the right person. It is easy to ask a few simple questions in Messenger, outside of a "public" post in the group.

When I first began to use Facebook Messenger, I quickly figured out it was like having a personal assistant that recorded everything. I could start a conversation with someone who was interested and stop talking to them at almost any point. Yet I could go back and pick up the conversation without missing a beat. In fact, I could restart a conversation six months or a year later and still have the original discussion chain. That is priceless!

I come from a detail-oriented sales world where I took paper applications and always had to make sure I made good notes. Keeping track of them and knowing when it is time to contact someone back is a TON of work if you aren't organized and detail-oriented! If you have been in sales longer than 10 years, or if you have been involved with companies less technologically advanced, then I'm sure you know what I mean!

Using Facebook Messenger eliminates the need to do those things. You can initiate a plan, setting reminders for you to call a prospect back at a set date and time. You can read back through Messenger and refresh your memory about a prospect's particular situation.

The information is right there, and available for all to see. There are many ways to see the easy benefits. I had a possible client reach out to me eight months after our initial conversation because her bankruptcy time limit was up. She was ready to become a homeowner!

Much like the rest of Facebook, Messenger keeps improving with added options and changes to features that don't work as well. It is such a valuable communication tool for us now, especially with the tracking system we use to help the loan originators, processors, and real estate agents to see the current stage of the loan process. By changing each group Messenger picture to represent the current loan stage it is easier for us to see what we have going on at a glance.

THE BUZZ LOOP

Facebook Messenger Groups

Homes Color Code

Red House = anyone that's been pre-screened and is or has filled out an application.

We name these groups: Loan Officer First Name/Client Name/Start
Example: Neil/Bob Smith/Start

Yellow House = Anyone you have talked to who is sending in documents.

We name these groups: Loan Officer First Name/Client Name/Docs Otw
Example: Neil/Bob Smith/Docs Otw

Purple House = Anyone you screen and need to TBD approve because of their situation.

We name these groups: Loan Officer First Name/Client Name/TBD
Example: Neil/Bob Smith/TBD

Orange House = Anyone who is given a pre-approval letter. (you can go from red to orange)

We name these groups: Loan Officer First Name/Client Name/Pre-Approved
Example: Neil/Bob Smith/Pre-Approved

Grey House = Anyone who does not meet minimum requirements for a loan, not credit based.

We name these groups: Loan Officer First Name/Client Name/Hold
Example: Neil/Bob Smith/Hold

Blue House = Anyone who needs credit repair.

We name these groups: Loan Officer First Name/Client Name/Repair
Example: Neil/Bob Smith/Repair

Green House = Contract on the house is in!!!

We name these groups: Loan Officer First Name/Client Name/Contract
Example: Neil/Bob Smith/Contract

"When you learn to communicate with the Buzz Loop, you can carry on more conversations than ever! And life will get much easier with far fewer phone calls."

Marty Human

MOVING FORWARD & THE BUZZ LEVELS

Communication keeps getting better, and I wanted to find a way to get all the real estate agents and loan originators to jump in and participate. We created six status levels to reach based on the number of members in their PBGs and the number of groups they joined as a goal formula to follow.

We told everyone about the new levels and described a positive and motivational system to feel good about their position, see their accomplishments with us, tracking the leads and applications all the way to funded loans. We explained how easy it is to post in all the different groups from the comfort of home, and how they now have a way to BRAND themselves with Facebook groups.

We showed how effective using Facebook Messenger is by utilizing it in a way many people didn't even realize was possible! Then we made it even better by adding in badges for the different levels of group accomplishments. It became easy for us to really see who was participating once we started using the level badges.

Kickstart to **FORWARD FORCE**

To achieve the first level, you must reach at least 100 members in your Personal Branding Group, and also join at least 100 other local groups. This level can be accomplished fairly quickly for most people, especially if they aren't shy about adding friends and previous clients.

It definitely doesn't hurt to add any and all previous clients you can find. You can even call up some of those old clients and have them send you a friend request on Facebook.

You could also just send a little message that says, "Hello, yoohoo, remember me? We closed on your home loan four years ago." Just keep it light and friendly!

The response you receive will probably be something like, "Well, of course I remember. How are you?"

Always try to keep that rapport going, then say, "I'm creating a Facebook Group for my previous clients, friends, and family. So, if you come across anyone needing a real estate agent or loan originator, feel free to go ahead and give them my number, and also add them to my Homes for Sale group."

This is important, because if you only hand them your business card or phone number, there is a strong possibility you will never be called. However, if you put them in the group, they will see your posts more frequently and their friends will see some of your posts as well.

You will always have a closer attachment to that person than if you just exchanged numbers. When the day comes that they do get approved, then BOOM! You now have another client ready to go! Once you have reached this level, it's on to the next!

Moving up with MOMENTUM MOVERS

In order to reach the next level, you must get to 500 members in your Personal Branding Group. As a MOMENTUM MOVER you will really start see your group begin to grow more, especially if you do a good job of sharing your group and keeping the activity going.

It is very important that you learn how to set up the shortcuts for text replacements on your phone, especially when it comes time for sharing in groups and messaging! Having these shortcuts set up changed everything for me because it simply made my job SO MUCH EASIER!

Before you know it, you will have MASS EFFECT

Our third level is called MASS EFFECT. To reach this level you must have 1,000 members in your Personal Branding Group. Once you reach this level, you will notice a lot more activity in your group, especially if you let other agents in and they share their listings.

One of these days you will be very glad that you put in the effort to grow your business, and I truly believe in my heart that groups are the BEST way to reel in business. They're also the best way to BRAND yourself, and they're the best way to stay in contact with all of your previous and future clients. Your group will grow, almost by itself!

You will develop a constant stream to pull business out of, and you will build a connection with people that will last as long as you want it to. The more you keep feeding new information, activity and people into your groups, the more you will get out of them.

The ENERGY keeps gaining and you achieve VERTICAL SPEED

Once you have hit 2,500 members in your Personal Branding Group, you will be at the point where you have far more people interested in your business than ever before. They will even be HELPING you grow by recommending you to their friends, family, and even complete strangers they see posting who might need your kind of expertise!

You want to make sure you continue to post interesting content in your Personal Branding Group and keep engaging with your members on a daily basis. The more activity in your group, the more it will grow with new members who request to join. The more members that request to join your group, the more opportunities you will have to find out exactly who needs your services!

You have reached new heights when you hit MOONWALKER

At this point you will have 5,000 members in your Personal Branding Group! It is a huge advantage to have your own personal group and to have CONTROL of the advertising and content provided to your followers.

They will be your personal group of people who want to see YOU succeed, and they will HELP you by RECOMMENDING you! This happens because Facebook routinely shows our friends the groups and pages that we are interested in that they think our friends might also be interested in. This is part of the algorithm in the news feed everyone scrolls through.

If you keep doing more on Facebook to interact, you will get more rewards out of it because you will be shown to more people. You WANT TO MAKE SURE that you keep adding new friends, and that you keep looking at, commenting on, and liking new things on Facebook.

And then, FINALLY, you will be part of the ROYAL BUZZ!

This is the ultimate! When you reach 10,000 members in your Personal Branding Group, you will have approximately 50-100 new people requesting to join EVERY SINGLE DAY! It will happen without even having to advertise that you have a group!

At least 50-100 people will be requesting to join your group and seeing your three questions every day. After you have approved their membership in the group, you can begin to interact with them in a way that was never possible before. And your name will be out there as an option for people buying, selling, or refinancing a home—far more effectively than if you were door knocking or making phone calls!

You will have more business than you could have imagined possible, and it flows directly to YOU! I have people reaching out to me saying, "Hey, I am up to X number of members in my group". They all say how amazing it is to have the ability to run a group and ask three questions to anyone who wants to join! There are a ton of opportunities to utilize the Facebook Groups and gain more business and we keep discovering more options EVERY DAY!

We have already had real estate agents and brokers say that they will no longer waste money on leads because we taught them how to get applications without having to make a single phone call. They have realized that growing their PBG is not HARD work. They can even just share their group in some other groups, and add a message that says, "Please join and share." Soon enough people will start sharing the group, and then their friends re-share, all while new people are still requesting to join.

You can also go inside your Personal Branding Group and create special things for members to do, such as "Add a Friend Friday." Or you can have one of the questions for potential members read, "Would you be willing to add five or more friends or family members to this group to help us grow?" Almost all the time, the answer will be, "Sure, no problem!" You usually won't be able to track if they've actually added five people, but the intention behind this question is to help your group grow faster.

I was unsure how I was going to get every one of the on the same page. Kristi gets the credit for developing a system to help motivate and track everyone on the team. With our system, you will be able to hire a personal assistant to keep track of all of this for you, or you can do what a lot of us do and put your kids to work, LOL. They are more tech savvy than we are. You can also teach them how to post for you!

"You will never be in enough Facebook Groups, so keep joining every day. Kamikaze Kristi is currently in over 4,000 Facebook Groups, and most of them are in just a few different states."

Marty Human

BUZZ NATION FACEBOOK GROUP & BUZZ TEAM HELP

One group we created, called Buzz Nation – Real Estate Agents & Loan Originators – Making Home Owners – Buzz LOOP, is for our loan originators and agents who are working together. Real estate agents in the states that we operate in can ask to join this group as well.

Another great group for agents or loan originators (based in any state or country) is: Real Estate Agents & Loan Originators – FB Group Marketing Made Easy By Marty Bahama. This group will allow you to network with thousands of agents and loan originators.

Buzz Team Members are invited to a members-only Facebook Group, Buzz Team - Real Estate Agents and Loan Originators (Official), where I do Facebook Live training five nights per week and our Buzz Team members share their tips and tricks with the group. They can also join an awesome group for content to use in their PBGs, Personal Branding Group Content for Buzz Team Members, where Buzz Team members share ideas for posts.

We create a secret Messenger group for each one of our members to have access to the Buzz Team for support. I personally chat with members and answer questions when in a welcome introduction call. They get ZOOM training, access to our information and videos inside of the Google Classrooms, and help with creating and growing the perfect Personal Branding Group.

Our Buzz Team Group has also created a great referral avenue for real estate agents. They are introducing themselves to each other and sharing some of the creative ideas that are working for them in the groups. Anytime agents pick up a client who will be buying in a different area, they simply go inside the group and say, "Hey, who wants a client looking for a house in La La Land?" It is an easy way to earn even more money without having to do much. I know agents in out-of-state groups earning a decent amount each year just off of referral bonuses.

We do change things up sometimes, but we have been running a Facebook Live episode on Monday nights called "The Buzz Formula". In this great Live, the gorgeous Kamikaze Kristi joins me to help teach and motivate our Buzz Team Members. We talk about the success everyone is having and give suggestions to members who have questions with how to respond to some of their messages.

We like to joke around and quite often we will burst out various song lyrics. We recently decided (referencing the movie "The Matrix") that Kristi is "The Oracle" of Facebook Groups and I am "The One". We also reference some rap music and MGK - I have been playing the "APP DEVIL" and since she is really the "APP GOD".

One thing these Facebook Groups will do is keep you as busy as you want or need! It's pretty simple, if you want more business you post more. If you are too busy, you post less. It's really a bit addictive and fun to connect with so many people. For the real estate agents and loan originators who have already become part of Buzz Nation, there is no longer stress about acquiring new clients. They all say, "Thanks to the Buzz, I will never pay for advertising again."

"Once you have hit 10,000 members (Royal Buzz) in your Personal Branding Group, you will be at the point where your group will do almost all the work finding clients for you."

Marty Human

MARTY HUMAN

THE BUZZ QUICK START

Rule #1: LEARN HOW TO USE TEXT REPLACEMENT (explained at the end)

Rule #2: Always START DISCUSSIONS and NEVER use pictures in your post. You should also avoid the Marketplace.

Rule #3: When REQUESTING to join groups, always join as a person, not a real estate agent or loan originator. If you answer the questions by saying you are either of these two professions, you will often not be allowed into the group.

Rule #4: Do everything in MODERATION with both the Facebook Groups and Messenger, and never too fast. (This will help you avoid Messenger Timeout and Facebook jail)

For immediate results, follow these simple steps:

While in Facebook, click the top search bar and look for local buy/sell/trade groups within your area, with at least 5,000 members. No matter where you are, there are thousands of them. Once you have joined at least 10 groups, drop the pre-set post listed below. Always click the button called START DISCUSSION, make sure you post in 10 Facebook

Buy/Sell/Trade Groups with more than 5,000 members, AND DO NOT ADD OR TWEAK THIS POST:

> Looking for applicants for our Renters to HOMEOWNERS PROGRAM? Requirements: 2 years employment (doesn't have to be same job). Like/Comment below if you would like information. STOP RENTING and START OWNING!

It really is that simple! (The post above has worked all over the world, not just the USA).

Step One: Start joining Buy/Sell/Trade Groups

Join 10 to 20 Facebook Groups (Buy/Sell/Trade) each day in the local areas you want to prospect and try to target groups that have 5,000 members or more. The more groups you join, the better! You can never be a member of too many groups, so join more every day!

If you join ten groups daily, it won't take long to become a member of hundreds of Facebook Groups. The hundreds of thousands of people who are homeowners or looking to become homeowners are right there, at your fingertips!

The best Facebook Groups to join are buy/sale/trade, yard sale, clique, or hip groups. For example, I have pulled many loans out of Hip Nashville. These types of Facebook Groups have tons of members, increasing your chances of finding new clients. You generally want to avoid the very specific ones such as, automotive/church/sports/alumni type groups.

Step Two: Start posting in the Facebook Groups USING TEXT REPLACEMENT

Post in 10 Facebook Groups at Noon, 3pm, and 7pm with your preset post (written above) and rotate it through your different groups daily (totaling around 30 posts per day).

Always START DISCUSSIONS without pictures. It took us four and a half years of research to learn that posting without pictures generates better response from possible clients. It appears as if you're trying to share some helpful information, instead of advertising to sell a product. This allows them to trust you, so go ahead and advertise without advertising!

You will get three types of possible clients from these posts:

1. The people that LIKE your post! Maybe they are just window shopping and not in any hurry to move.

2. The people who COMMENT on your post! These people need to be messaged directly. Next, go back to the post, LIKE their comment, and reply with "PM sent".

3. My favorite people are the ones who message you directly. We call these possible clients EAGER BEAVERS. Immediately find out if they have a house picked out and are ready to go! These are the people who really want to buy and will take the necessary steps to get there.

When it comes to joining groups and posting, do both in moderation. Also, make sure to get in the habit of paying attention to all the notifications rolling in because you want to respond quickly just in case your post is deleted.

Step Three: Responding to your three types of clients.

Immediately send a friend request (or at the very least "add" them on Messenger).

MARTY HUMAN

Send them a PRIVATE MESSAGE, "Thanks for liking (or commenting) on my post, where are you at in the home buying process?" Most people fall into the category of "just getting started" or "I have a house picked out."

The goal is to have a DIRECT connection with this person in Messenger who is possibly interested in buying or selling a house. The people who get the best results make sure to ask lots of open-ended questions and direct the conversation towards the ultimate end goal.

It is very important to remember what really gets "The Buzz" started. This happens when you go back to the post where they commented "info". Replying back with "PM Sent" lets others see that you are a real person, and they will be curious about what information you were providing. The next thing you know, you will have a few hundred comments on that one post.

Step Four: Find out their direction.

After they respond, figure out the best direction to go, depending on the response. There are three main directions for you to send them: Ready Today, Ready Over Time, or Credit Repair.

1. Ready Today: If they are trying to get pre-approved, ask them some basic pre-qualifying questions such as: Do you have at least a 580-credit score and two years full time job history? If they answer yes, message them a link to your application, if you are the loan originator, or if you are the real estate agent then send the client your loan originator's application link. Use The Buzz Loop to make this magic happen.

2. Ready Over Time: Assess their situation, send them an application link, and give them a game plan to move forward. If they are waiting several months, for example if they are stuck in a lease, in the short term you can get them prepared to gather information and documents. Set a reminder to reach back out to them when it's time to move forward. Make sure they are in your HOMES for Sale PBG.

3. Credit Repair: If they say they have bad credit, you may want to direct them to credit repair. Feel free to send them to anyone who is reputable and set a reminder to reach back out in 4-6 months.

For Loan Originators:

When you reach out to the client, ask them the "Gauntlet" questions below. Typically you will get an idea quickly about the situation they are in from the answers they give right here. This is where we "weed the good from the bad."

Do you have two full years of employment?

What do you think your credit score is?

Do you have three active credit tradelines (car, bank loans, credit cards), or three alternate tradelines (cell, electric, water, cable, insurance, etc.)?

Have you had a bankruptcy or foreclosure?

Do you have any student loans?

Do you pay child support?

Do you have a down payment? 401k, etc.

Once you get them "sold" on the loan, you will want to create a Facebook Messenger group. Include your team at this point by clicking on that client's name, and when the list of options pops up you will "create Facebook Messenger group."

THE BUZZ FUTURE

I am on a mission to help some of the 87% of real estate agents who do not make it in the first few years, along with helping all the struggling loan originators out there. I love helping people that are struggling and need more volume, more employees, or maybe more applications, and want to learn how to bring them in the easy way. Sign up to become a Buzz Team Member and we will help you be more successful. We have posts that are proven to find buyers and sellers. We continually develop new polls to generate interest. We have multiple response variations. Everything we teach is easy to REPLICATE.

Our branch is a top performer, and we are at this level without paying for advertising or leads. Real estate agents and loan originator friends across the WORLD, between myself and our amazing Buzz Team members, we will teach you how to drive the Facebook Groups like a Lamborghini! We recently created 5 Google Classrooms which provide a path to follow with all the information and videos to help you understand the steps to take in order to succeed. Some of the most valuable topics include text replacement, how to buy the Facebook Groups and to find them for FREE!

You will pick up more business from the comfort of your own home and have the freedom of living the rest of your life without worrying when your next client will appear, or how much money it's going to cost for the next lead. I have been very fortunate, because I know there are places out there that don't allow the use of social media to make connections or have that old school mentality about Facebook and Messenger. If you are frustrated, or if you have questions about the possible options, reach out to me. I can give you some personal advice and start teaching you (and your team) the Buzz Formula. When you work with us you are part of the Human Energy Buzz Team family.

It's not always easy, especially when people try to tell you it won't work. But the fact is, it is definitely possible to follow what we have been successfully doing. Make it work so well that people start asking you, "HEY, WHERE ARE YOU FINDING ALL THESE CLIENTS?" Then you can tell them, "Marty Bahama, aka MMFH, and Kamikaze Kristi showed me The Buzz Formula, and now I'm covered up with clients thanks to the Facebook Groups!"

Call or text me anytime, 865-360-0048, and let's talk about it!

NAMES TO KNOW

When I got back in the business, the requirements for becoming a licensed Mortgage Loan Originator meant that I needed to take an approved course and pass an exam, and I used My Mortgage Trainer. It is where I have continued to refer anyone who is interested in becoming a loan originator. They are a great company to use for both initial license training and continuing education (CE). They really go out of their way to serve their clients and go the extra mile to support you. You can learn more about the licensing or CE requirements for your state by visiting their website at https://www.mymortgagetrainer.com.

Kim White is a Branch Manager, and happens to be a great friend of ours, along with her crazy (and supportive) husband Jeff. Many thanks to both for testing the waters and being one of the first to try the Buzz Formula! Kim is one of the best miracle workers I know when it comes to closing those tougher loans. Reach out to her if you need an amazing lender in TN, IN, or MI.

Real estate agents, look out for Buzz Formula Nation to SWEEP the world one day. Tristea Bankston, a super agent and wonderful person, helped spark this idea. Feel free to look her up on Facebook and reach out to her anytime. Thank you so much for being such a big Buzz believer and putting out an amazing video for us. You will find Tristea anywhere from Tullahoma to Nashville. She is amazing and will help you find your dream home.

One of our SUPERSTAR real estate agents, Michael Hicks is knocking on that "BEST" door. He has turned so many renters into homeowners, it's crazy, and he reeled them in from the Facebook Groups. You will find Michael in the Jackson and Dyersburg, TN area. Thank you for working the Buzz Formula and always participating in my Facebook Lives each night.

Annie Smith, thank you for being one of our most dedicated Buzz Team Members and for referring so many people to us. You are such an amazing and sweet person. We will always appreciate everything you have done!

Cori Perez, thank you for being one of the biggest Buzz supporters ever. You have introduced more people to The Buzz than anyone else so far, and you most certainly hold the record for being first on our Buzz Lives.

Tomeka Purcell, one of the most amazing Buzz Team stories we have, was on the hot seat at her company for not producing enough applications until she met us. She is now averaging 12 applications per day, has her own office, and a secure money-making career. Thank you so much for believing.

Jen Overstreet, thank you for the amazing videos and all the Buzz clients you have helped become homeowners. Making dreams come true, you really are an amazing person. Find Jen in Gallatin and Nashville TN.

Rob Hernandez, thank you so much for introducing us to the tool that picks up Facebook Groups abandoned by Admins. Real estate agents and loan originators have picked up hundreds of Facebook Groups for FREE. If you are out in Austin TX, be sure to look Rob up.

David Sanders, thank you for sharing the video from the rooftop of Steak & Shake, when you left there as a manager to be a full-time real estate agent, thanks to the Buzz Formula! You and Keith Nitsch make a great team. Anyone reading this in Cleveland, TN, be sure to look them up.

Landon Martin, thank you for being so awesome and dedicated to the Buzz. Landon and Missy Truitt have been battling it out to see who can pick up the most Groups for free or buy the most! Every day it seems like they are picking up a new one containing thousands of members.

David Whalley, thank you so much for holding the Number One spot for the best SELLER'S POST, which reeled in 57 possible sellers in a seven-hour period. Also, thank you for believing in the Buzz! Look David up if you are in Savannah, GA.

Ronald Dayley, thank you for being so great at using The Buzz Formula to reel in listings. Ron is in the Clarksville, TN, area and currently leading all the Buzz Team members with the number of members in his Personal Branding Group.

Jill Lemery is a Buzz Team loan originator, ready to make you a homeowner in VA. She closed three loans from the very first post she dropped!

Raffy Ilano, thank you for meeting me in Knoxville. It was great chatting in person with a Buzz Team Member using the Buzz Formula in the Philippines!

Here is a handful of other real estate agents who are having great success using the Buzz. There are so many awesome people out there and hopefully we will get an opportunity to mention more of you in the next book! Thank you to Rina Seidel, Asad Shaikh, Carrie Gunnels-Lichon, Eric Montoya, Terri Wright, Alejandra Paladino, Carolina Seaver, Juan Carlos Lopez, Stacy Smith, Antonio Rosa, JC Young, Michael Dean, Cassandra Churchill, Joanne Simonelli, Laura Bur, Mirzah Ahmad, Bill Fischer.

Joseph Manual Gonzalez is a real estate agent and marketer extraordinaire, one of the best, so get connected with him. I recommend very few coaches but he's a great one and truly cares about helping people succeed.

You can reach out to any of the many branch managers, loan originators and loan assistants who are using the Buzz Formula and showing the world how to get things done! Corina Nicole (love your DRIVE), Rob Mapes (thank you for the energy), Jason Wojtyna (Buzz Formula Nation sir, thank you), Patty Dennehy (making her famous), Ra'Chelle Graham (rising superstar in SC), Adiel Hemingway (thank you, buddy), Shellie Carter (awesome lender in New Jersey), Jack Cooter, Melissa Karner (love your energy and dedication to the Buzz), Bev Davenport, Dennis Delaney, Val Nuttall, Mike Reber, Sean Beaudry, Joe Lovrek, Jason Maxam, Josh DeBlase Kyle & Lauri Mazeikas, Kevin Wheeler, Alfredo Robles, Rick Wamsley, Thomas Phillips, thank you all for believing in the Buzz.

Also, request to join the Facebook Group: New Real Estate Agents. This amazing group is run by Jennifer Penry Romano. It has over 40K real estate agents and loan originators. It's great group of people you can connect with and learn from others around the world. Jennifer, thank you for being so helpful to the Buzz.

I have met a lot of great Realtors & Loan Originators out of that big Real Estate group including Vinesa Gomez. She is a Buzz member as well and a wonderful person, former loan originator - now a Branch Manager, who covers AZ, CO, TX, CA, NV, OR, and WA with other states on the horizon.

"Buzz Team member and real estate agent, David Whalley, came up with the best seller's POST which reeled in 57 possible home sellers in seven hours - including their names, numbers, addresses, and home values! Three of those homes were valued around $1.5M!"

Marty Human

ACKNOWLEDGEMENTS

Thanks to all our Buzz Formula Nation friends and family.

Mom & Dad (Sonny & Velma Human), love you both dearly, thank you for everything!

Kristi's Mom and Dad, and family (Brenda & Bob Robillard, Dan, Sherry, Ben, and Crystal), love you all and thank you so much!

Kristi Human (Kamikaze Kristi), I will never be able to express enough how I truly do love you and how much you really changed Eryka's and my entire life. You always find a way to make everything better. How did this shark go fishing and catch the most perfect mermaid? I'm the luckiest man ever: 5-10-15. The Kristi and Marty Show Forever! You are the most beautiful woman on Earth.

Eryka Human (Pineapple) I couldn't have asked for a more perfect daughter. Very proud of your drive to get better and better at ASL. You are such a great person and that is what matters most in this life. I love you so much and you will always be my little baby. 11:11 wish time! Thank you Tiffany Huebner (Coconut) for being a great friend to Pineapple.

Justin Demers (J-Dog), for some reason you have liked me from day one. I have watched you grow over a foot taller in four years and I love you like you're my own. Thank you for being such a great kid and putting up with me. And a HUGE thank you for teaching me so much about the hyper cars.

David DeWitt (Diamond Dave DeWitt), for being a great partner and keeping me in line! A huge thanks for training our loan originators and the one million lunches you have bought for the office.

John Baker (Mr. President), working with us as our most dedicated and longest serving loan originator. More importantly, thank you so much for all your help with training and helping with our loan originators and processors.

Neil Mangrum, thanks for commenting on my post looking to borrow some cornhole bags. Being friends so long, I'm really enjoying working with you to build our branches. Thank you again for putting those awesome training manuals together.

Krystian Blackwell, you are getting a huge THANK YOU in my book because you broke my record for most applications in one day and I am so impressed with how fast you have taken off with the Buzz and mortgage industry!

(Tropical) Tim McGee, thank you for being the biggest Buzz Team Believer on Planet Earth, besides Kristi and myself. I'm very happy you showed up at the perfect time for both of us. Friends for life, buddy, thank you again for everything.

Jessica Lyn Davidson, thank you for working so hard helping the Buzz Team, our branches, and myself. Most importantly, thank you for putting up with me.

Dawn Marie, we are glad to have you helping us with the Buzz, thank you so much for all the effort you have put in as well.

Susan Hatfield, Cindy Kelley, Rachel Rayburn, Kandi Herron, for being wonderful processors and an amazingly supportive team. We couldn't be this successful without all of your help!

On the ultimate adventure with the family.

"Check out www.humanenergybuzz.com and become part of BUZZ FORMULA NATION."

Marty Human

www.humanenergybuzz.com

Facebook Groups are great for business, even beyond Real Estate! We would like to say thanks to everyone, and mention a few of the other businesses we have helped with The Buzz Formula as well.

Reagan Williams (MBM Heating & Air), is a long-time friend of mine and poker buddy and is a great example of the difference a Personal Branding Group (PBG) will make, even in a small town. He created a Business Page and after two years he had just over 600 likes. After creating a PBG for him, the group grew to over 1,500 members, and increased his business so much that he was able to hire more employees.

Lee Daugherty (Daugherty's Cleaners) Knoxville & Crossville locations. Thank you for letting me create your Personal Branding Group. It was awesome to see it have such an immediate effect to increasing business!

Jeremy Martin "Sheds", thank you for believing in the Buzz. He is showing plenty of people that he can sell a ton of sheds using The Buzz Formula.

I have known Amber Latrece for many years, thank you for showing us how to sell cable/internet using The Buzz Formula.

Special thanks to Dan Bell, we appreciate you always being there.

Watch out for our next book,

"The Buzz Formula:

Facebook Group Marketing for Everyone"

And make sure to let all your friends and family know, if they have a business they want to grow, they NEED to check us out!

Thank you so much for reading my book!

Let's connect on

@HumanEnergyBuzz